Population

Detecting Bias

Curriculum Consultant: JoAnne Buggey, Ph.D.
College of Education, University of Minnesota

By Neal Bernards

Greenhaven Press, Inc.
Post Office Box 289009
San Diego, CA 92198-9009

Titles in the opposing viewpoints juniors series:

Advertising
AIDS
Alcohol
Animal Rights
Causes of Crime
Child Abuse
Christopher Columbus
Death Penalty
Drugs and Sports
Elections
Endangered Species
The Environment
Forests
Free Speech

Garbage
Gun Control
The Homeless
Immigration
Nuclear Power
The Palestinian Conflict
Patriotism
Pollution
Population
Poverty
Prisons
Smoking
Television
Toxic Wastes

The U.S. Constitution
The War on Drugs
Working Mothers
Zoos

Cover photo: Hornback/Impact Visuals

Library of Congress Cataloging-in-Publication Data

Bernards, Neal, 1963-
    Population: detecting bias / by Neal Bernards; curriculum
consultant, JoAnne Buggey.
       p. cm. — (Opposing viewpoints juniors)
    Includes bibliographical references and index
    Summary: Presents opposing viewpoints on overpopulation, its
causes, its possible effect on the earth, and whether it should be
controlled.
    ISBN 0-89908-622-5 (acid free paper)
    1. Population—Juvenile literature. 2. Population—Economic
aspects—Juvenile literature. 3. Population policy—Juvenile
literature. [1. Population. 2. Critical thinking.] I. Buggey,
JoAnne. II. Title. III. Series.
HB883.B47   1992
304.6—dc20
                           92-17419
                              CIP

CONTENTS

An Introduction to Opposing Viewpoints

When people disagree, it is hard to figure out who is right. You may decide one person is right just because the person is your friend or a relative. But this is not a very good reason to agree or disagree with someone. It is better if you try to understand why these people disagree. On what main points do they differ? Read or listen to each person's argument carefully. Separate the facts and opinions that each person presents. Finally, decide which argument best matches what you think. This process, examining an argument without emotion, is part of what critical thinking is all about.

This is not easy. Many things make it hard to understand and form opinions. People's values, ages, and experiences all influence the way they think. This is why learning to read and think critically is an invaluable skill.

Opposing Viewpoints Juniors books will help you learn and practice skills to improve your ability to read critically. By reading opposing views on an issue, you will become familiar with methods people use to attempt to convince you that their point of view is right. And you will learn to separate the authors' opinions from the facts they present.

Each Opposing Viewpoints Juniors book focuses on one critical thinking skill that will help you judge the views presented. Some of these skills are telling fact from opinion, recognizing propaganda techniques, and locating and analyzing the main idea. These skills will allow you to examine opposing viewpoints more easily. The viewpoints are placed in a running debate and are always placed with the pro view first.

Detecting Bias

In this Opposing Viewpoints Juniors book, you will learn to detect bias.

All people are biased in favor of certain things and against others. For example, if you have favorite friends or relatives, it might be very hard for you to find fault with them, even when they do something obviously wrong or unkind. On the other hand, someone you particularly dislike might not be able to do anything right in your view. We do not always see things in an impartial, open-minded way. Our personal observations can be biased by what we like, dislike, or believe.

Similarly, authors of books, articles, and speeches are biased in favor of or against a particular point of view. Identifying an author's bias is an important critical thinking skill. Being able to detect the author's bias will help you determine whether the author is presenting an argument in a fair, objective manner or whether he or she is unfairly biased in favor of a particular view.

Many times bias, or point of view, is based on personal experience. For example, the owner of a corner convenience store often expresses her bad opinion of young people. She suggests that young people are thieves and are not being brought up right by their parents. She feels this way because she has caught young people stealing in her store. Although she has a reason for her bias, it is still a bias. Most of the young people she eyes with suspicion will not steal.

Sometimes bias is influenced by what parents or others in authority teach us. For example, members of the Ku Klux Klan believe blacks, Jews, and certain other minorities are inferior beings. They teach this bias to their children.

Sometimes bias is influenced by political events. For example, during World War II, the Japanese attacked an American military base. After this event, Japanese Americans were rounded up and sent to prison camps because officials feared they would act as spies against the United States. This decision was biased. Government officials treated all Japanese alike, even though many of them had lived in the United States and been loyal citizens for decades.

There are many other reasons people may be biased. In some cases, the reasons may seem like good ones. But biased statements must be carefully examined: Is the author's opinion based on objective information, or is it based on bias? How do you know? What reasons or evidence is used to support the statement? Do the reasons or evidence seem sound?

The authors of the viewpoints you will read in this book may be biased because of personal experience or for other reasons. Each author will try to persuade you that his or her opinion is correct. In order to figure out whether you will accept the author's opinion, you should attempt to discover whether the author is presenting the case fairly or with bias. Be aware of the author's point of view. What stand is he or she taking on the issue? Why would he or she take such a stand? Does the writer express fear, anger, or other strong feelings when describing his or her position? How do these emotions influence the objectivity of the viewpoint? Does the author use loaded words or phrases, that is, words that are overly positive or negative, to persuade you? Keep these questions in mind when analyzing the viewpoints in this book.

We asked two students to give their opinions on overpopulation. Both students are biased. As you read, attempt to identify their biases.

I think the world is overcrowded.

There are too many people in the world. We now have over five billion people living on this small planet, and that's too many. The earth can't support that many people. There's not enough food, fuel, or water for everyone.

Look at huge, dirty cities like Mexico City and New Delhi. People live like animals there. Millions of poor people in those cities live in terrible conditions with no food, running water, or electricity. They dig through garbage dumps for food.

When I went to Mexico City, I had to wear a mask to filter out the polluted air. Beggars also kept coming up to me, asking for money. It's crazy to argue that the world is not overcrowded when you see cities like that.

I do not think the world is overcrowded.

The world is not overcrowded. There is plenty of room left for the population to grow. If you fly over the western United States, you see hundreds of miles of open space where very few people live. When you get to California, the most populous state in the country, you see that people are living very well. California is not crowded and poor like Mexico City and New Delhi.

Even cities like Hong Kong and Tokyo are not overcrowded. A lot of people live there, but almost everyone has enough to eat and a place to stay. Third World cities only seem overcrowded because their governments are cruel and corrupt. They steal food and money that is sent from industrialized countries to help the poor. Their cities wouldn't seem overcrowded if the governments would do more for the people.

John and Ellie have very different opinions about population. Both of them are biased toward a particular point of view.

John:

POINT OF VIEW (bias)

The world is overcrowded.

LOADED WORDS AND PHRASES USED TO SUPPORT HIS VIEW

Look at *huge, dirty* cities like Mexico City and New Delhi. People *live like animals* there.

PERSONAL EXPERIENCE THAT REINFORCES HIS VIEW

John believes his visit to Mexico City proves that Third World cities are overcrowded.

CONCLUSION

John believes the world is overpopulated.

Ellie:

POINT OF VIEW (bias)

The world is not overcrowded.

LOADED WORDS AND PHRASES USED TO SUPPORT HER VIEW

Third World cities only seem overcrowded because their governments are *cruel* and *corrupt*.

PERSONAL EXPERIENCE THAT REINFORCES HER VIEW

Ellie flew over the United States and saw vast open spaces, convincing her that the world is not overcrowded.

CONCLUSIONS

Ellie does not believe the world is overcrowded. She believes there are other reasons for poverty and hunger.

In this sample, John and Ellie both express bias when presenting their viewpoints. Based on this sample, who do you think is right about population? How might your bias affect your opinion?

CHAPTER 1

PREFACE: What Effect Will Overpopulation Have on the Future of Humanity?

Overpopulation occurs when too many people live in an area that cannot support them. For example, experts consider some areas in China and India to be overpopulated because many residents do not receive enough food or are homeless.

The problem of overpopulation is of great concern. Experts predict that the world's population will grow rapidly in the next fifty years. In 1650 there were only 550 million people on earth. In 1990 there were 5.3 billion, or ten times more. According to most predictions, world population will double to ten billion by 2040.

Population researchers like Anne Ehrlich and Paul Ehrlich of Stanford University call this trend a "population explosion" and think it is alarming. They argue that world economies and food producers will not be able to support these large populations. If overcrowding continues, the Ehrlichs predict that both jobs and food will become scarce. This will lead to mass starvation, poverty, and death.

Others, however, do not share their concern. Researchers like Karl Zinsmeister, formerly of the American Enterprise Institute in Washington, D.C., argue that while it is true that more people use more resources, they also replenish resources by working and producing. People, Zinsmeister claims, contribute to the world economy and help build the future. They grow food, they plant trees, and they make products in factories. For example, Tokyo is a crowded city of eight million people. However, it is not considered overpopulated because the people of Tokyo work hard. Though it has few natural resources, Tokyo has enough money to buy whatever it needs from other cities and other countries. Zinsmeister believes that cities like Tokyo are good illustrations of how people can find ways to solve population problems.

Discussing population and its effect on the future is controversial. When making points about population, people often use biased arguments. Careful readers should be aware of bias in an author's viewpoint. Watch for bias as you read the next two viewpoints.

Overpopulation threatens humanity's future

Editor's Note: In the following viewpoint, the author argues that overpopulation threatens humanity's future. He maintains that more people will mean less work, food, and housing for everyone. Follow the questions in the margin. They will help you identify the author's bias.

The author compares the world's future to the Third World, an extreme comparison that reveals his bias. Since many parts of the world do not have a population problem, this comparison is not objective.

The Ehrlichs seem to share the author's point of view. By quoting only those who agree with him, the author makes his argument less objective.

Overpopulation is one of the gravest threats humanity faces. It threatens to destroy poor countries, cripple developing nations, and severely damage rich countries. Third World nations already display the effects of overpopulation. These countries are polluted, crowded, poor, and disease ridden. If the population continues to grow at the present rate, the entire planet will look like the Third World.

From 1930 to 1976 the world's population doubled from two billion to four billion people. According to population experts Anne and Paul Ehrlich, the population will double again every thirty-two to thirty-nine years. World leaders are not prepared for this kind of expansion. They have no idea how to create enough work and grow enough food for the coming wave of people. World leaders already have their hands full with the problems of today. What will happen when those problems are magnified by billions of additional people?

The Ehrlichs believe the effect of overpopulation will be "more frequent droughts, more damaged crops, more famines, more dying forests, more smog, more disease, more gridlock, more drugs, and more crime."

So far the world has not been hit with the full effects of population growth. But in the future, the world's population will explode. Mexico City is a good example. In 1950, less than four million people lived in Mexico's capital city. Now more than nineteen million people call it home. That is a five-fold increase in just forty years! The city's population grew because of an extremely high birth rate among the poor people who lived in the countryside nearby. These people could not find work in the country, so they moved to Mexico City. Since the poor tend to have more children than other people, the population quickly swelled. This type of gross overcrowding could happen anywhere work becomes scarce, including rich cities like Los Angeles, Paris, or London.

Overpopulation will lead to massive unemployment. There will be little work for poor, uneducated people in the future. Third World nations will have to create 800 million new jobs by the year 2000 to employ everyone. That will not happen.

If people cannot work, they cannot feed themselves or their families. Without jobs they will have little access to health care. With the number of unemployed people reaching into the millions, the problems of overpopulation will compound. The results will certainly destroy Third World nations through disease and hunger.

Already, the disastrous effects of overpopulation are evident in many Third World cities. Open sewers, lack of food, and dirty living conditions abound. There is not enough space, food, or work for everyone. As a result, disease spreads easily. In Bangladesh, parents do not have enough money to give their children shots against illness. World Bank figures show that only 2 percent of the children in Bangladesh are protected against common infectious diseases. Without protection, disease spreads rapidly through poor, crowded communities. If there were fewer people, the problem would not be so bad.

The threat of overpopulation is very real. Each day the world's population increases by 260,000 people. Our planet simply cannot handle such rapid growth. Overpopulation threatens to overwhelm humanity before many realize that it is a problem. As an editor for the *Washington Spectator* warns, "The need is to open the eyes of humanity to an impending doom before it is too late."

Here the author reveals his bias by using statistics that support his argument and loaded terms like "gross overcrowding."

Worst case scenarios are often used in biased arguments. What terms does the author use that prove he is not presenting his case objectively?

The author claims that overpopulation is to blame for illness. What facts does he use to support his case?

Is overpopulation a world threat?

The author writes that population growth is a serious problem. What proof does he give that overcrowding is harmful? Does the author use loaded words when presenting his view? If so, how do these words reveal the author's bias?

Overpopulation does not threaten humanity's future

The predictions are wrong: overpopulation does not threaten humanity's future. If anything, population growth is good for the world because it provides more workers and more minds to discover answers to society's problems.

What does Eberstadt call the Ehrlichs' predictions? Is this a biased description of their work? Why or why not?

People who argue that population is out of control are like Chicken Little saying the sky is falling. It is not happening. For example, Anne and Paul Ehrlich's predictions that overpopulation will cause widespread famine and war have not come true. Their population forecasts are less accurate than astrologers' predictions in supermarket tabloids. Nicholas Eberstadt of the well-respected American Enterprise Institute says the Ehrlichs base their theories on pseudoscience, or fake science. He calls their predictions "modern witchcraft."

"Chicken Little" and "The Boy Who Cried Wolf" are children's stories. These comparisons ridicule people who disagree with the author and reveal the author's bias.

If anything, during the last twenty years of rapid population growth, world conditions have improved. In 1968 Paul Ehrlich wrote that India would never be able to feed itself. Yet today India not only feeds itself, but sends food to other countries! Ehrlich's warnings now seem like the boy who cried wolf. They have not come true. No one should believe his gloom and doom predictions since so few of them have come true.

The author presents the arguments of Zinsmeister, who agrees with him, in a very positive way. How might this reveal the author's bias?

A more knowledgeable population researcher named Karl Zinsmeister writes that the world's standard of living has improved greatly since 1960. He notes that life expectancy, or how long people can expect to live, has increased in Third World countries from forty-two to sixty-one years. The number of doctors in these countries has more than doubled and the caloric intake of the average Third World citizen has risen by 20 percent. This means that poor people now have more access to health care than they did in 1960. It also means that enough food exists to feed everyone. Zinsmeister's research proves that it is ridiculous to argue that the world cannot support a growing population.

How does the author describe the Dutch? Indians? Does he admire one over the other?

The world offers ample evidence that population growth does not lead to starvation. Crowded living conditions do not have to mean disease, poverty, and starvation. Look at the Netherlands, for example. There, the population density is 354 people per square kilometer. India, which we are often told is overcrowded, has only 228 people per square kilometer. Yet the Dutch enjoy a great standard of living because they are creative, hard-working, and educated. East Indians, on the other hand, suffer from poor education, a rigid caste system, and a lack of leadership. The problem is not that there are too many people, but that the quality of people in certain areas is not very good. The Netherlands has millions of intelligent, skilled workers and India does not.

In well-run countries, people are assets. In poorly run systems, people are burdens. For example, in Korea and Japan people are viewed as producers. There, political leaders welcome population growth because it means more workers in the factories, offices, and on the farms. By allowing people to attain good educations and decent jobs, the Japanese and Koreans have created efficient, productive societies.

It is time to stop listening to the naysayers like the Ehrlichs and listen to the reasoned opinion of people like Zinsmeister and Eberstadt. Much of the world is not overcrowded, it is simply poorly run.

The author uses Korea and Japan as examples of countries that successfully cope with their population problems. Do you know of other countries that do not? By using only examples that support his argument, the author is hoping to persuade readers to accept his point of view.

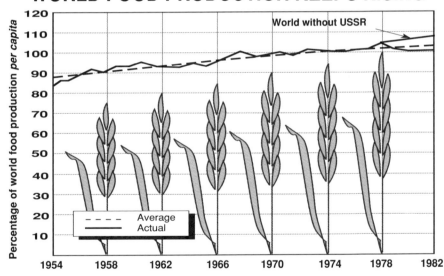

WORLD FOOD PRODUCTION KEEPS RISING

1969-1971 = 100 (excluding Peoples Republic of China). World food production per capita.

Source: *Theory of Population and Economic Growth*, Julian L. Simon, 1986. Basil Blackwood Ltd., 108 Cowley Rd., Oxford OX4 1JF, Canada.

Is there a future?

Why does the author believe the future will be better? Give two examples of words the author uses to describe people who predict coming population catastrophes. How do these words reveal his bias?

CRITICAL THINKING SKILL 1 Detecting Bias

After reading the two viewpoints on overpopulation's effect on the future, make a chart similar to the one made for John and Ellie on page 8. State each author's point of view, then list any examples of personal experience (either the author's own personal experience or the personal experience of the people quoted) that might bias his or her view. A chart is started for you below:

Viewpoint 1:

POINT OF VIEW

LOADED WORDS AND PHRASES USED TO SUPPORT AUTHOR'S VIEW

"educated, hard-working people"

"poor, ignorant couples"

PERSONAL EXPERIENCE THAT REINFORCES AUTHOR'S VIEW

CONCLUSIONS

Viewpoint 2:

POINT OF VIEW

LOADED WORDS AND PHRASES USED TO SUPPORT AUTHOR'S VIEW

"modern witchcraft"

"ignorant political leaders"

PERSONAL EXPERIENCE THAT REINFORCES AUTHOR'S VIEW

CONCLUSIONS

After completing your chart, answer the following questions:
1. How do you think the authors could have made their arguments more objective, less biased?
2. Even after recognizing the author's bias, which argument did you find most convincing? Why?

CHAPTER 2

PREFACE: Can World Resources Support a Growing Population?

An ongoing problem with population growth is finding enough food, clothing, shelter, and jobs for everyone. As cities and nations grow, they need more resources to support their people.

Certain environmental experts, like Lester R. Brown, president of a research center called the Worldwatch Institute, do not think the earth's resources can support additional growth. Brown writes that the world's average annual grain harvest has increased only 1 percent since 1984, while the population has grown by almost 10 percent. He notes that air pollution, acid rain, and global warming have made it more difficult for farmers to satisfy the world's hunger. Brown, like many others, believes that only a limited supply of food, oil, and water exist on earth. He does not think population growth can be supported forever on these finite resources.

Others contend that the world's resources are limited only by people's imaginations. They argue that science will find a way to feed, clothe, and shelter humanity. Science, they believe, will discover new ways to save energy, build housing, and improve methods of farming. A study by the International Institute for Energy Conservation states the United States could save almost two million barrels of oil a day by raising the fuel-efficiency of cars to 45 miles per gallon. And with advanced farming techniques, Mexico could further improve its grain harvests, which already quadrupled between 1950 and 1980. These signs of scientific improvement and conservation cause many scientists to believe that resources can keep up with continued population growth.

The next two viewpoints debate whether science can support an ever-growing population. As you read, look for bias.

Natural resources can support more people

Editor's Note: In the following viewpoint, the author contends that natural resources can support at least forty billion people. He argues that science and discovery will easily feed the world's growing population. Look for examples of bias in his argument.

The world's population has been growing since the beginning of human existence. For hundreds of years people like nineteenth-century economist Thomas Malthus have said humanity would one day run out of resources because of population growth, but it has never happened. The world's resources, along with human science and imagination, have continued to support a growing human population.

Julian Simon, a world-famous economist, contends that population growth will actually help increase resources. Rather than worrying about the future, Simon has a very positive outlook. He writes, "The more people, the more minds there are to discover new deposits and increase productivity, with raw materials as with other goods."

Simon's educated view is shared by many other scientists. They argue that increased demand creates increased supply. When more people demand more food, water, and housing, companies will work harder to find new resources and conserve existing resources. They will think of better, more efficient ways to build products. To prove his theory, Simon notes that U.S. cars improved their fuel efficiency from 13.1 miles per gallon in 1973 to 17.9 miles per gallon in 1985, cutting gasoline consumption by 20 billion gallons a year.

Why does the author only quote experts that agree with him? How could the author make this viewpoint more objective in this case?

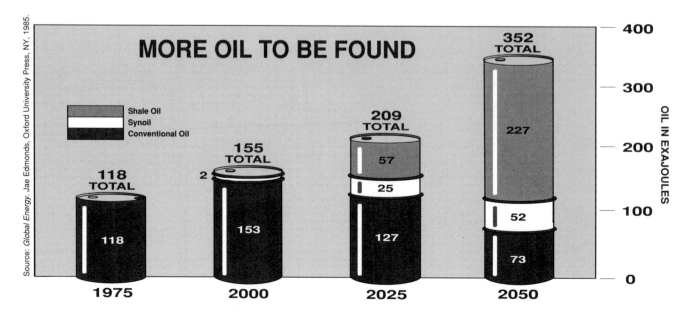

Source: *Global Energy,* Jae Edmonds, Oxford University Press, NY, 1985.

MORE OIL TO BE FOUND

Shale Oil
Synoil
Conventional Oil

OIL IN EXAJOULES

118 TOTAL — 118

155 TOTAL — 2 / 153

209 TOTAL — 57 / 25 / 127

352 TOTAL — 227 / 52 / 73

1975   2000   2025   2050

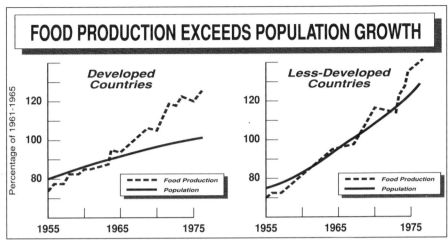

FOOD PRODUCTION EXCEEDS POPULATION GROWTH

Developed Countries

Less-Developed Countries

Percentage of 1961-1965

- - - - Food Production
—— Population

Source: Bernard J. Nebel. *Environmental Science*, Prentice-Hall, Englewood Cliffs, NJ 07632.

Scientists who believe the world's resources are running out are shortsighted. They mistakenly believe we will continue to exploit gas and oil reserves at an increasing rate. They also think farmers will destroy the land until no more food can be produced. These negative scientists do not believe people are smart enough to change to meet new circumstances. History has proven otherwise.

When buffalo almost became extinct, U.S. leaders passed laws to protect them. When strip mining of coal threatened to permanently deface the land, companies stopped the process. When farmers learned that their crops were sapping nutrients from the land, they rotated their plantings and added fertilizer. For example, during the "Green Revolution" (1945-1990), the world's total food output tripled while the population only doubled. There is no reason food output cannot triple again in the next thirty-five years.

People have the imagination and intelligence to make good choices about natural resources. Imagination and science will allow humanity to stretch existing resources to supply everyone. As Philip C. Cruver, president of Titan Energy Limited, writes, "Technological advances and the genius of the human spirit will keep America's lights on in the future while respecting the limits of nature."

List the loaded terms in this paragraph. What type of bias do they reveal?

Though an author may show bias, he can also use reason to make his point. This paragraph uses reasoned statements.

The author could easily have made this a less biased essay. Which words would you eliminate to make it less biased?

Can the masses be fed?

What does the author think of scientists who believe in a prosperous future? Find three words the author uses to describe these scientists? What do these words reveal about the author's point of view?

Natural resources cannot support more people

Editor's Note: In the following viewpoint, the author states that world resources cannot support a population explosion. He does not believe science will be able to keep up with the overwhelming demand for food, clothing, and shelter. Answer the questions in the margin to help you detect the author's bias.

Do the examples prove that the world's resources are running out? How does this indicate the author's point of view?

Can you detect the author's bias toward science? What is it?

How does the author characterize people? Why is this biased?

How does the author describe the state of farming today? Does his description seem objective, or tainted with bias? How can you tell?

As the world's population grows, it becomes more and more difficult to feed, clothe, and provide shelter for everyone. Witness the ongoing starvation in Ethiopia, the shortage of food in what was once the Soviet Union, and even the lack of water in prosperous California. Overpopulation threatens to drain the world's resources until nothing is left.

It would be nice to think that science and imagination are enough to provide for the world's needs, but they are not. As most respected scientists agree, there are only a certain number of natural resources to exploit. They are called non-renewable resources. Non-renewable resources include oil, gas, and all minerals such as aluminum, copper, and iron ore. Once gone, these resources can never be replaced.

To prove that science and imagination are not enough, one need only look at the United States. It contains only 5 percent of the world's population, but it consumes 30 percent of the world's energy. Science and technology has not helped the United States increase its resources. The more developed the United States becomes, the more resources it uses. People buy cars that burn gas. They purchase stereos and televisions that require energy. They live in homes that require heating. Science is more geared toward making people use more, buy more, and throw away more. If people rely on science to save society, they are in trouble.

The reason science will never save world resources is that people are selfish. Rather than thinking about long-term conservation, people would rather have large cars, fattening food, air conditioning, and loud stereos. Most people are not willing to sacrifice comfort to preserve resources for future use.

Even renewable resources like timber and agriculture cannot meet future needs. Farmers are already pushing their fields to the limit. The British magazine *South* reports that because of poor farming techniques and topsoil loss, 14.8 million acres—an area the size of Ireland—is turned into unproductive desert. Rather than expanding farmable land, we are shrinking it. The land that is lost cannot be replaced. Don Nardo, author of *Population*, debunks the myth that farmers can find more land to grow more food. He writes, "Human beings already use or abuse most of the world's available land."

As most people know, the world's forests are quickly disappearing. The rain forests of Brazil are being slashed and burned to make way for grazing cattle. Once these rain forests are gone, they can never be replaced. *Development Forum* notes that "timberland equal to the size of California will vanish by the end of the century." What will future generations use to make paper and build houses if we cut down all the forests?

Selfish car owners continue to pollute the air. Large industries pollute the water. And lazy Americans pollute the land through their mountains of garbage. The world cannot handle a few billion more polluters. Scientists who argue that the world contains enough resources should breathe the air in Mexico City, drink the water in India, or wade through the garbage on Staten Island in New York. Our fragile earth cannot, and will not, support more people.

What loaded words are used in this paragraph? How might they bias the reader?

Paul Conrad, © 1974, The Times. Reprinted by permission of Los Angeles Times Syndicate.

Will there be enough?

What is the author's view of human nature? What does he think of Americans? How do his views influence his opinion that the world is running short of resources?

CRITICAL THINKING SKILL 2
Detecting Bias

This activity will allow you to further practice identifying bias. The paragraphs below focus on the subject matter of this book. Read each paragraph and consider it carefully, deciding whether the author is biased. Read the statement following the paragraph and select the best answer to complete it.

If you are doing this activity as a member of a class or group, compare your answers with those of others. You may find that some have different answers than you do. Listening to the reasons others give for their answers can help you in identifying bias.

EXAMPLE: Citizens of the United States, while making up only 5 percent of the world's population, selfishly consume nearly 30 percent of its fuels. To save precious resources, Americans must stop driving their gas-guzzling cars.

The author of this paragraph
a. reveals a bias against Americans.
b. takes no sides.
c. thinks everyone must conserve resources.

ANSWER: a. reveals a bias against Americans.

1. The threat of overpopulation is a major concern for many Third World nations. Even leaders in cities like Tokyo, New York, and Los Angeles have revealed a concern for overcrowding. These leaders realize that the issue of how to handle population growth must be dealt with on an international level.

The author of this paragraph
a. blames Third World leaders for overpopulation.
b. tries to remain objective.
c. blames industrialized leaders for overpopulation.

2. The threat of overpopulation has been greatly exaggerated. Population analysts who tell alarming stories do so only to increase their fame. It is much more exciting and interesting to say that overpopulation threatens to ruin the future than to correctly say that science can handle further growth.

This author expresses a bias against population critics. Which of the words and phrases used above best shows the author's bias?
a. population analysts.
b. greatly exaggerated.
c. exciting and interesting.

3. Many people want to control population by handing out birth control devices to every young woman. What they forget is that birth control is forbidden by some religions. Giving birth control devices to a devout Catholic would be like telling a Hindu to eat a cow (which they consider taboo) or telling a devout Jew or Muslim to eat pork (which they consider a sin).

The author of this paragraph
a. supports distributing birth control.
b. takes no sides.
c. opposes distributing birth control.

4. We are wrong to put our faith in science. Scientists said that planes could never fly, rockets would never reach the moon, and that human bodies could not endure running marathons. Scientists now say that we have enough food and resources for forty billion people. Do not believe them. They have been wrong before.

The author of this paragraph
a. has a bias against scientists.
b. shows no bias.
c. has a bias in favor of scientists.

CHAPTER 3

PREFACE: What Causes Overpopulation?

In the population debate, poor nations blame rich nations for taking their natural resources. In turn, rich nations blame poor nations for having too many people.

Leaders of many poor nations claim that wealthy, industrialized countries like the United States use more than their fair share of resources. World Bank statistics support this idea. According to these statistics, the United States consumes 30 percent of the world's fuels while having only 5 percent of the world's population. Third World leaders argue that developed countries exploit and impoverish poor nations by using up their resources. They point out that people in industrial nations drink most of the world's coffee, which is grown in poor Central American and African countries. Leaders of Third World countries claim that cropland used to grow food for the rich nations could be better used to help feed the natives.

Others counter that people in poor nations should blame themselves for overpopulation since they are the ones having too many children. According to Dr. Nafis Sadik of the United Nations population program, nine of every ten new babies are born in Third World countries. Governments of many Third World nations do little to slow the high birth rate, even though such nations lack resources to support more people, critics contend. The strain on world resources, it is argued, comes from this uncontrolled population growth.

This issue is hotly debated. People on both sides often hold strong biases. See if you can detect this in the next two viewpoints.

Editor's Note: In the following viewpoint, the author writes that the blame for population problems rests with the poor. Look for bias in the author's statements about the poor.

How have the author's travel experiences influenced his opinion?

These statistics are provided by a conservative magazine. How might they be biased?

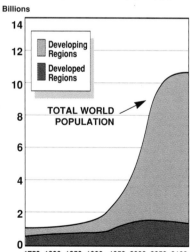

WORLD POPULATION GROWTH: 1750-2100

Billions

Developing Regions

Developed Regions

TOTAL WORLD POPULATION

14
12
10
8
6
4
2
0

1750 1800 1850 1900 1950 2000 2050 2100

Source: Population Reference Bureau estimates, 1990.

For those who have visited overcrowded cities in poor Third World countries, it is easy to see why these nations have an overpopulation problem. The poor live huddled together in filthy slums with more children than they can support. By continuing to have large families, the world's poor are bringing population problems on themselves.

The poor have been allowed to overpopulate the earth because the death rate in Third World nations has been dropping while the birth rate has remained high. Advances in health care have allowed more Third World babies to survive. While this is good news, it also means that more people are living into adulthood and draining the world's resources. Meanwhile, the birth rate for developing countries continues to soar.

For example, statistics provided by the *Washington Spectator*, a conservative magazine, show that populations in Africa and Latin America are growing too fast for these nations to support the growing number of people. By 2025, 1.1 billion more people will live in Africa, three times the number that lived there in 1985. Latin America will add 374 million by then, almost double the 1985 number. Both regions are quite poor. Food is already scarce in these areas. The only way for both regions to avoid disaster is to drastically reduce their birth rates soon. As Anne and Paul Ehrlich write, "Rapid population growth in the poor countries has outstripped their ability to grow more food."

With population growth rates high, it is impossible for people to get the food, education, and job training they need to become productive members of society. Instead, the malnourished and untrained poor will continue to perform poorly paid manual jobs or, worse yet, they will have no jobs at all. If poor people had fewer children the young would have a better chance of getting the food and education they need.

The poor are too shortsighted to realize that they cannot feed all their children. In the Third World, people mistakenly believe that more children mean more workers, thus more money and food. This idea worked at one time when most people were farmers. However, this theory no longer holds true when most people live in large cities. Now, more children mean more people competing for a limited number of jobs. The poor have become a drain on the world's resources.

Whom does the author blame for overpopulation? Could the statement have been made more objectively? How?

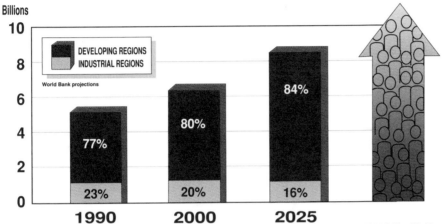

POPULATION SURGE IN THE THIRD WORLD

Billions

DEVELOPING REGIONS
INDUSTRIAL REGIONS

World Bank projections

1990: 77% / 23%
2000: 80% / 20%
2025: 84% / 16%

Source: Rodolfo Bulatao et al., *Europe, Middle East, and Africa (EMN) Region Population Projections, 1989-90 Edition*, World Bank, Population and Human Resources Department, Washington, D.C., working paper series 328, November 1989.

A common trait shared by most of the world's poor is their religion. Most are either Catholic or Islamic. Not surprisingly, both religions encourage large families and discourage birth control. The poor's blind belief in these religions contributes to population problems.

Is the author's opinion of religion objective? Why or why not?

Lest we blame only the Third World poor, the poor in the United States also contribute to the overpopulation problem. A reporter for the *Washington Spectator* writes about an experience the mayor of Washington had. While inspecting a homeless shelter, the mayor was confronted by a woman who asked for a better place to live. The woman had fifteen children. How can population problems be solved if the poor continue to have this many children?

Does this example bias your opinion toward homeless people? Why or why not?

The poor are to blame for overpopulation problems. Until they stop having so many children, starvation, disease, and overcrowding will continue.

Who is to blame?

The author believes the poor and their religious beliefs are to blame for overpopulation. Do his statements reveal a bias toward religion. What loaded words does the author use when describing the poor?

Editor's Note: The author of the following viewpoint argues that wealthy nations are to blame for overpopulation. He contends that the rich have kept the Third World poor by stealing their natural resources and giving little in return. Watch for biased phrases and answer the questions in the margin.

Is the author's opinion of wealthy nations objective? Why or why not?

"Exploit" is a loaded term that reveals the author's bias.

The politics of poverty and overpopulation are hard to understand, but blaming the poor is not the answer. One can hardly blame the poor for having nothing. Instead, it is the rich who are responsible. Wealthy nations, by taking valuable resources from poor nations and giving little in return, are to blame for population problems.

After all, why are many Third World nations unable to feed themselves? Because they are feeding us. In countries like El Salvador and Nicaragua, for example, coffee and bananas take the place of needed crops like corn and wheat, which could be used to feed the local population. Coffee and bananas are grown because they receive good prices on the international market. They are also grown because much of the farmland is owned by American or European companies. The banana and coffee plantation owners know that land and labor prices are much cheaper in Third World countries. Rather than pay American or European farmers a higher rate, they exploit the Third World poor and take their produce. Luxury items for wealthy nations take the place of staple foods, causing the struggling natives who work the fields to go hungry.

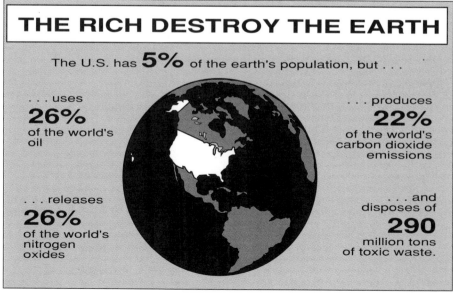

THE RICH DESTROY THE EARTH

The U.S. has **5%** of the earth's population, but . . .

. . . uses
26%
of the world's oil

. . . produces
22%
of the world's carbon dioxide emissions

. . . releases
26%
of the world's nitrogen oxides

. . . and disposes of
290
million tons of toxic waste.

Source: Worldwatch Institute.

The rain forests of South America are being destroyed for similar reasons. Enterprising farmers have no use for the rain forests, so they cut them down and use the land to raise cattle. The farmers sell the cattle to Japan and the United States, leaving their countryfolk hungry. Land that could support hundreds of South Americans is used instead to feed a handful of meat-eating wealthy people. It is the selfishness of overfed people in developed countries that causes starvation in poor nations.

Developed nations also exploit poor countries for their timber rights. The Philippines has lost more than 90 percent of its original forest cover due to logging. In 1985 Indonesia banned the export of logs, a $3 billion a year business, because their forests were disappearing. Japan, the world's largest user of tropical timber, was buying the logs as fast as they could be cut, with little regard for the environment.

Some people argue that the money paid for these natural resources helps poor nations buy food and other necessities. Unfortunately, this is not true. In general, the money paid for wood, minerals, and coffee goes to a few wealthy landowners in each country. The landowners often invest this money in foreign countries, rather than using it to help the natives. The landowners work closely with business leaders in the industrialized world to exploit the poor. Those who toil on the land generally receive little for their efforts.

The poor are not to blame for overpopulation. Rather, it is the rich people's greed and their resulting actions that cause population problems in Third World countries.

How does the author use statistics to support his bias toward wealthy nations?

Is the author's opinion of landowners biased? How can you tell?

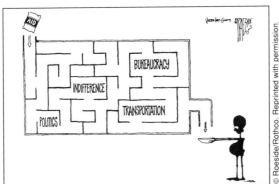

© Roeside/Rothco. Reprinted with permission.

The real cause of poverty

How does the author describe residents of wealthy nations? Do you detect any bias in his terms? Why or why not? Compare these to the terms used to describe the poor. How do they differ?

Throughout this book, you have seen cartoons that illustrate the ideas in the viewpoints. Editorial cartoons are an effective and usually humorous way of presenting an opinion on an issue. Cartoonists, like writers, can be biased in presenting their opinions. In this activity, you will be asked to detect the bias in the cartoon pictured below.

There are several terms used in the cartoon with which you may be unfamiliar. The term "food sufficiency" that floats just above the water refers to a country's ability to feed itself. The people pictured in the cartoon are shown as being well below the ability to feed themselves. "Economic development" refers to the hope that once a country reaches self-sufficiency its economy can grow.

1. What does the cartoonist think is keeping poor countries from reaching food sufficiency and economic development?

2. Look at the couple pictured standing beneath the water. Why do you think they are portrayed in torn clothing? Who does the cartoonist think is to blame for overpopulation?

3. What other elements in the cartoon reveal the cartoonist's bias?

4. For further practice, look at the editorial cartoons featured in the daily newspaper. Try to identify the biases in the cartoons.

'We can't seem to keep our heads above water' . . .

CHAPTER 4

PREFACE: Are International Family Planning Programs Needed?

Family planning programs teach couples to control the number of children they have. Usually, family planning involves providing education and birth control. The issue of family planning can be very controversial.

For example, many people in industrial nations believe family planning should be forced on people in developing Third World countries. They argue that in order to receive money or food from industrialized countries, Third World nations should initiate strong family planning programs. These people reason that family planning would help Third World nations reduce the number of malnourished, unwanted children. Relieved of the burden of feeding so many children, Third World nations would have a better chance of developing their economies.

Opponents of forced family planning believe the policy is racist. They contend that family planning is only suggested for non-white cultures. They also criticize family planning for ignoring that members of the Catholic, Islamic, and Buddhist faiths are forbidden to use family planning. They say family planning is only a thinly veiled attempt to maintain political control over poor nations by not allowing their numbers to grow.

Opponents of family planning believe there are better ways to reduce population growth than to force Third World people to use birth control and abortion. They recommend economic development and better education as ways to reduce population growth.

The next two viewpoints discuss whether family planning is needed. Watch for bias in the authors' statements.

International family planning programs are needed

Editor's Note: In the following viewpoint, the author maintains that family planning programs are needed to control population growth. He argues that education and birth control will prevent women in poor nations from having more children than they can support. Watch for biased adjectives or arguments the author may use.

What does the author think will happen if family planning is not used? Why does this conclusion reveal the author's bias?

World leaders must find a humane solution to the population explosion, or a solution will find itself. That solution could be widespread famine, starvation, and a war for resources. Without family planning, the world could find itself losing millions of people to the devastating effects of overpopulation.

The core of any worldwide family planning program should be education about birth control. Third World parents need to be taught that they must limit childbearing for their own good. The late anthropologist Margaret Mead wrote, "Birth control is the only humane and rational answer to our population dilemma." This famed scientist knew better than anyone what was needed to slow the world's growth and to improve the world for everyone.

THE SUCCESS OF CERTAIN FAMILY PLANNING PROGRAMS

Country	TOTAL FERTILITY RATES*		% Change
	1960	1987	
Singapore	6.3	1.6	-75
Taiwan	6.5	1.8	-72
S. Korea	6.0	2.1	-65
Cuba	4.7	1.8	-62
China	5.5	2.4	-56
Chile	5.3	2.4	-55
Colombia	6.8	3.1	-54
Costa Rica	7.4	3.5	-53
Thailand	6.6	3.5	-47
Mexico	7.2	4.0	-44

* AVERAGE NUMBER OF CHILDREN PER WOMAN

Source: 1960 data from Ansley Coale, "Recent Trends in Fertility in Less Developed Countries," *Science*, August 26, 1983; 1987 data from Population Reference Bureau, 1987 *World Population Data Sheet* (Washington, D.C.: 1987).

Consider that in some poor countries, like the west African nation of Senegal, the average woman gives birth to 9 children. Most families in Senegal live in filthy squalor from lack of food, money, and work. Their disastrous birth rate will quickly strangle any hope the country has of becoming healthy. Likewise, a high global birth rate will drag down any economic improvements that might be in the making. For there to be a healthy future, the overall birth rate must drop to 2.2 children per family. Right now the rate remains above 3 children per family.

To reach this goal, family planning programs must educate young, unschooled mothers and provide them with birth control. Health workers must go into poor communities to teach the people how to care for their children, how to stay healthy, and most of all, how to use contraceptives.

The encouraging news is that women want more information about and methods of birth control. The Agency for International Development (AID) reports that it needs 100 million more condoms to meet the demand. The sad news is that AID has neither the condoms nor the money to buy them. Because of this shortage, many women who want birth control cannot get it. A report published by Zero Population Growth states that 77 percent of the married women in Africa who want no more children are not using contraception, either because they cannot get it or they do not know how to use it. The duty of wealthy, educated nations is to give these women reliable birth control methods and the knowledge to use them. According to United Nations statistics, if that can be done, the birth rate would drop 27 percent in Africa, 33 percent in Asia, and 35 percent in Latin America.

By investing a few million dollars in family planning, nations could save billions of dollars and thousands, if not millions, of lives. Better family planning leads to fewer children. Fewer children leads to more food and jobs for everyone else. More work and more food means better health, more money, and a chance for Third World nations to rise from poverty. Strong, well-funded family planning programs are needed immediately. It is the best way to reduce a population that is bursting the seams of our small planet.

Does the author's selection of Senegal as an example indicate bias? Why? Why not?

AID relies on the public's money to survive. Do you think this fact might bias their statistics?

Zero Population Growth works to reduce the birth rate. Why might their information be biased? Why not?

This viewpoint was written by a man. Do you think his gender influences his opinion about family planning? Why or why not?

Point of view

The author writes that women need to be educated about having fewer children. What does he write about men? Does this lack of information reveal a bias? Do you think the viewpoint would be different if written by a woman? Explain your answers.

International family planning programs are not needed

Editor's Note: In the following viewpoint, the author states that better living conditions are needed to solve the problems associated with overpopulation. He believes the poor's basic needs should be met before money is spent on birth control.

Four out of every five people live in developing countries. One out of every four people in developing countries lives in abject poverty. That amounts to one billion people. These one billion people are so poor they can neither work nor get enough food to remain healthy. Among the extremely poor, fourteen million children die from hunger and disease each year. They do not die from overcrowding or a lack of birth control, they die because their government cannot provide food and their economy cannot support more jobs. They die because Western leaders do not care. Family planning is not the answer to solving the problems of overpopulation. The answer is economic and political change.

Millions of the world's poor suffer from malnutrition, a lack of basic health care, and the opportunity to work. None of these problems are related to overpopulation. They are related to poverty. The poor are poor because their governments make bad economic decisions, their nations lack natural resources, and their nations are exploited by industrial countries. Ethiopia's poor suffered from the war between the communist government and the rebels. El Salvador's poor suffer because their best land is used to grow coffee and bananas for the United States. Nicaragua's poor suffer from a lack of natural resources and a history of unstable, corrupt governments. These nations do not need family planning. They need money to help their economies.

Instead of helping the poor escape poverty, developed nations call for family planning programs. Family planning takes the focus away from real issues like economic development and basic health care. It also takes away the guilt that the members of First World nations should feel about worldwide poverty. It allows the wealthy to blame the victims.

Even the alleged success stories of family planning need to be questioned. Family planning programs have done little to raise the standard of living in poor nations. Thailand is such a case. Its birth rate dropped 47 percent from 1960 to 1990. The average number of children per woman fell from 6.6 to 3.5. Advocates of family planning consider the lowered birth rate a great success. But is it? Researcher Frances Moore Lappé does not think so. She notes that more than half

Does the author use a reasoned argument to explain the causes of poverty? Explain your answer.

Is "alleged" a loaded term? How does it reveal the author's bias?

of Thai children under the age of five are still malnourished. Lappé, who founded Food First, a research center that investigates the root causes of hunger, writes, "Malnutrition has been increasing despite both lowered birth rates and improved food production." Family planning has done nothing to improve living conditions in Thailand.

Like the problems in many other nations, Thailand's problems do not stem from overpopulation, but from other factors. Those factors include overworked land, a lack of natural resources, corrupt leaders, and poor trade links with other countries. Family planning will not solve these problems. Money spent on such programs will be wasted. What is needed are social and agricultural programs to improve the lives of the poor. Teach them to farm, train them to work, give them proper food and clothing. Only then will they see the need for less children and reduce their family size. Donald Mann of *The New York Times* agrees and asks, "Are family-planning programs the answer to halting population growth? Clearly, they are not." Family planning programs that do not improve poor people's lives, Mann argues, are doomed to failure.

Food First is a health and nutrition organization. Would their statistics be biased? Why or why not?

This author's argument is more reasoned than many other viewpoints in this book. What makes his argument more reasoned?

BIRTH RATES ALREADY DROPPING

Natural Increase of Population 1965-1985

		1965	1980	1985-1990
Developing Countries	Middle East and North Africa	2.8%	2.7%	2.7%
	South Asia	2.5	2.2	2.2
	East Asia (excluding China)	2.6	2.3	2.1
	China	2.7	1.1	1.4
	Latin America and the Caribbean	2.8	2.5	2.1
Industrialized Countries		0.9%	0.5%	0.4%

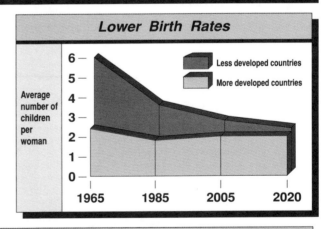

Lower Birth Rates

Sources: World Bank projections for 1985-1990 (left); Population Reference Bureau, United Nations (right).

Poverty and blame

Whom does the author blame for the Third World's problems? Does the author reveal a bias toward developed countries or Third World nations? Support your answer.

Detecting Bias in Statements

This activity will allow you to further practice detecting bias. The statements below focus on the subject matter of this book. Read each statement and consider it carefully. *Mark B for any statement that you believe is biased. Mark N for any statement you believe is not biased. Mark U for any statement for which you are uncertain.* Be sure to provide a reason for your answer.

If you are doing this activity as a member of a class or group, compare your answers with those of other class or group members. Discussing your answer with others may help you discover your own biases.

EXAMPLE: It is easy to see that family planning is needed to stop population growth before it is too late. Poor people are starving to death in every country already. And each major city has beggars, thieves, bums, and homeless people. We certainly do not need more babies.

ANSWER: B, bias. The author offers no firm statistics in favor of family planning and uses loaded terms like "beggars," "thieves," and "bums."

1. Many people are surprised to learn that our global resources continue to expand. Food production in the United States is now five times higher than in the 1940s. And new reserves of oil and natural gas are continually being discovered.

   Answer_____ Reason_____

   _____

2. Humanity's future looks bright because science continues to make advances. Buildings are now built higher, cars go farther on a gallon of gas, industries produce goods more cleanly, and people live longer because of better health care.

   Answer_____ Reason_____

   _____

3. Americans are not the only ones to blame for overcrowding and starvation in Third World nations. Other selfish countries include Japan, which exploits its poor neighbors in Southeast Asia, and Germany, which takes valuable natural resources from many African nations.

   Answer_____ Reason_____

   _____

4. China and Cuba have done an amazing job of reducing their birth rates. While their tactics were not always humane, they were very effective.

   Answer_____ Reason_____

   _____

FOR FURTHER READING

The author recommends the following books and periodicals for further research on the topic. Check the works consulted list that follows for further suggestions.

E. Calvin Beisner, "Prospects for Growth: A Biblical View of Population, Resources, and the Future," *Christian Century*, December 19-26, 1990.

Chronicles , "Life on a Small Planet: The Politics of Population Growth," October 1991. Special issue on population.

Tyler Cohen, "Bedroom Call to Arms: Or How I Stopped Worrying and Learned to Love the Population Bomb," *Reason*, February 1988.

Nicholas Eberstadt, "Population Change and National Security," *Foreign Affairs*, Summer 1991.

Werner Fornos, "Population Politics," *Technology Review*, February/March 1991.

Robert W. Fox, "The Population Explosion: Threatening the Third World's Future," *Futurist*, January/February 1992.

Michael Fumento, "The Profits of Doom: How to Achieve Fame and Fortune by Being Spectacularly Wrong," *Crisis*, February 1991.

Eugene Linden, "The Last Drops," *Time*, August 20, 1990.

Stephanie Mills, "Population: Red-Hot Realities for a Finite Planet," *Garbage*, May/June 1991.

Don Nardo, *Population*. San Diego, CA: Lucent Books, Inc., 1991.

New American, "The Resilient Earth," June 1, 1992.

Will Nixon, "The Population Problem Is Not Just About People," *Utne Reader*, May/June 1992.

Nafis Sadik, "World Population Continues to Rise," *Futurist*, March/April 1991.

Julian L. Simon, "The More the Merrier," *Forbes*, April 2, 1990.

William K. Stevens, "Humanity Confronts Its Handiwork: An Altered Planet," *The New York Times*, May 5, 1992.

John Tierney, "Betting the Planet," *The New York Times Magazine*, December 2, 1990.

Utne Reader, "Ten Myths About Our Environmental Crisis," May/June 1990.

Ben J. Wattenberg, "The Birth Dearth: What Happens When People in Free Countries Don't Have Enough Babies?" *Population and Development Review*, March 1990.

WORKS CONSULTED

The following books and periodicals were used in the compilation of this book.

Lester R. Brown, Christopher Flavin and Sandra Postel, *State of the World, 1989*. Washington D.C.: Worldwatch Institute, 1989. This annual collection presents numerous statistics on population growth and other issues that affect the environment. Collection supports the theory that population growth is a problem that lowers the world's living standards.

Paul R. Ehrlich and Anne H. Ehrlich, *Earth*. New York: Franklin Watts, Inc., 1987. The Ehrlichs repeat their assertion that overpopulation is a serious problem that will eventually lead to humanity's downfall.

Paul R. Ehrlich and Anne H. Ehrlich, "The Population Explosion: Why Isn't Everyone as Scared as We Are?" *The Amicus Journal*, Winter 1990. Authors predict that the world's population will reach ten billion and more and will lead to famine, disease, and the depletion of natural resources.

Frances Frech, *Out of Africa: Some Population Truths*. Kansas City, MO: Population Renewal Office, 1988. Useful pamphlet that criticizes arguments that population growth damages the environment. Believes the problems in Third World countries are due to massive mismanagement in those nations.

Betsy Hartmann, "Bankers, Babies, and Bangladesh," *The Progressive*, September 1990. Author asserts that population control programs have hurt the Third World. They do nothing to solve the real problems of Third World poverty, unequal distribution and scarcity of resources.

Don Hinrichsen, "The Decisive Decade: What We Can Do About Population," *The Amicus Journal*, Winter 1990. Author argues that population growth is depleting natural resources. Advocates the use of international population control programs.

R. Cort Kirkwood, "The Population Bomb . . . Defused," *The Freeman*, November 1989. Author supports his argument that population is not a problem with lots of quotes from international population experts.

Francis Moore Lappé and Rachel Schurman, "Taking Population Seriously," *Food First Development Report No. 4*, September 1988. This article summarizes the viewpoint presented in the authors' book, *The Missing Piece in the Population Puzzle*. In it, the authors argue that hunger is caused by a lack of economic and political reform.

Ray Percival, "Malthus and His Ghost," *National Review*, August 18, 1989. Author argues that population growth improves living standards.

Washington Spectator, "Population, the Overflowing Bowl," September 15, 1988. Editors of this conservative journal argue that population growth is severely damaging the environment. Presents lots of useful statistics.

Zero Population Growth, "The Higher the Population, the Fewer the Options," *The Zero Population Growth Reporter*, August 1990. The national organization argues that overpopulation is largely responsible for environmental damage and that an aggressive, worldwide family planning campaign is desperately needed.

Karl Zinsmeister, "Supply-Side Demography," *The National Interest*, Spring 1990. Zinsmeister argues that the population explosion theory is incorrect and that population growth in the Third World is not the cause of its problems.

ORGANIZATIONS TO CONTACT

Institute for Food and Development Policy (Food First)
145 9th St.
San Francisco, CA 94103
(415) 864-8555

The institute provides research and education on world hunger and ecological issues. It believes that foreign aid is counterproductive and contends that world hunger can be eliminated if First World countries allow Third World countries to take control of their own food production. The institute publishes books, pamphlets, and a newsletter.

Population Council
1 Dag Hammarskjöld Plaza
New York, NY 10017
(212) 644-1300

The council conducts research and provides technical support and services around the world in contraceptive technology, family planning, and population-related policymaking. It publishes pamphlets and newsletters.

Population Renewal Office
36 W. 59th St.
Kansas City, MO 64113
(816) 363-6980

Opposes efforts to reduce the world's population. It maintains that the earth has the resources to support many more people. It further contends that a declining world population is more dangerous to human survival than overpopulation. It publishes articles and brochures.

Worldwatch Institute
1776 Massachusetts Ave. NW
Washington, DC 20036
(202) 452-1999

The institute serves as a resource center on topics such as population growth, depletion of the ozone layer, reforestation, and other environmental issues. Its publications include the bimonthly *WorldWatch* magazine and the annual *State of the World*. It takes the position that overpopulation is a serious global problem.

Zero Population Growth (ZPG)
1400 16th St. NW Suite 320
Washington, DC 20036
(202) 332-2200

ZPG lobbies to reduce population growth in order to ensure adequate resources and prevent environmental destruction. It publishes books and pamphlets.

INDEX

Africa
  overpopulation in, 22
Agency for International Development
  (AID), 29

Bangladesh
  effects of overpopulation on, 11
birth control
  education in
    as necessary, 28-29
    as unnecessary, 30-31
birth rates
  statistics on, 31
Brown, Lester R., 15
buffalo, 17

California
  lack of water
    as proof of overpopulation, 18
  overpopulation not a problem, 7
cars
  as source of environmental damage,
    19
  improvements in efficiency, 16
cash crops
  as cause of Third World poverty, 24
Catholicism
  as cause of overpopulation, 23
coal mining
  as example of successful conservation
    effort, 17
Cruver, Philip C., 17

Eberstadt, Nicholas, 12
Ehrlich, Anne and Paul
  predictions of, 9, 10
    criticisms of, 12
El Salvador
  as producer of food for the U.S., 24
  poverty in
    as caused by cash crops, 30
environment
  damage to
    overpopulation as cause, 15, 19
  effect of people on, 18
Ethiopia
  poverty in
    as caused by overpopulation, 18
    as caused by war, 30

family planning programs, 27
  as necessary, 28-29
  failures of, 30
  goals of, 29
Food First, 31
food production
  as limited, 18
  statistics on, 17

government systems
  as contributing to poverty, 13
grain harvests

statistics on, 15
green revolution, 17

Hong Kong, 7
  overpopulation not a problem, 7

India
  effects of overpopulation
    as not severe, 12
  social problems of
    as cause of poverty, 13
International Institute for Energy
  Conservation, 15
Islam
  as cause of overpopulation, 23

Japan, 13

Korea, 13

Lappé, Frances Moore, 30-31
Latin America
  overpopulation in, 22
life expectancy
  as improving, 12

Malthus, Thomas, 16
Mead, Margaret, 28
Mexico City
  as overcrowded, 6
  pollution in
    as caused by overpopulation, 11, 19

Nardo, Don, 18
natural resources
  effect of population on, 15
    as harmful, 18-19
    as minimal, 16-17
Netherlands, 12-13
New Delhi, 6
Nicaragua
  as producer of food for the U.S., 24

oil
  statistics on amount left, 16
overpopulation, 6-7
  as severe threat, 10-11
    con, 12-13
  causes of, 21
    Catholicism, 23
    lack of family planning, 28
    the poor, 22-23
    wealthy nations, 24-25
  definition of, 9
  effects of
    as harmful, 18
    on environment, 15
    on the future, 9
    poverty, 6
    unemployment, 11

people

as cause of environmental damage, 18
Philippines, 25
population
  effects of
    on natural resources, 15
    as harmful, 18-19
    as minimal, 16-17
population explosion, 9
population growth
  positive effects of, 12
  statistics on, 9, 22
poverty
  statistics on, 30

rain forests
  destruction of
    as caused by overpopulation, 19, 25

Sadik, Nafis, 21
science
  as solution to overpopulation, 15
Senegal, 29
Simon, Julian, 16

Thailand
  social problems of cause poverty, 31
Third World
  as overpopulated, 10
  effects of overpopulation on, 11
  family planning and
    should initiate, 27-28
  population statistics, 23
  poverty, 30
    causes of
      cash crops, 24
      insensitivity, 30
      internal governments, 7
      the poor, 22
      wealthy nations, 21
    women, 29
Titan Energy Limited, 17
Tokyo
  overpopulation is not a problem, 7, 9

United Nations
  population statistics, 29
United States
  as cause of poverty in Third World, 21
  as greedy consumer, 18
  cities of
    threat of overpopulation to, 11
  conservation statistics, 15
  overpopulation not a problem, 7

World Bank
  statistics on overpopulation, 11
Worldwatch Institute, 15

Zero Population Growth, 29
Zinsmeister, Karl, 9
  theories of, 12